IRISH TALES
AND SAGAS

When Cuchulain grew to be a man, he was the most famous of all the warriors of the Red Branch.

Ulick O'Connor

IRISH TALES
AND SAGAS

Illustrations by
Pauline Bewick

DRAGON
Granada Publishing

Dragon Books
Granada Publishing Ltd
8 Grafton Street, London W1X 3LA

Published by Dragon Books 1985

First published by Granada Publishing
in hardback in 1981

Copyright © Ulick O'Connor 1981
Illustrations © Pauline Bewick 1981

ISBN 0-583-30404-4

Printed and bound in Great Britain by
Collins, Glasgow

Set in Baskerville

Contents

The king's own room had bronze walls and a silver ceiling, on which were carved golden birds with eyes of shining diamonds. A silver rod lay always at Conor's feet with three golden apples on it. Whenever he struck the rod, all would be silent.

*T*he tales I am going to tell are mostly of the heroic age in Ireland. This was many hundreds of years before the birth of Christ. The strange thing is that, while many other lands were still in a barbaric state, there existed in Ireland a civilisation that had its own literature and music, its laws and history, and was ruled over by kings and princes.

The people that ruled Ireland in that distant time were the Celts. There are not, indeed, many races in Europe who do not have some Celtic blood in them. The French and the Germans are partially Celtic. So are those Spanish people who live in Northern Spain. Britain was first ruled by the Celts. The Brythonic branch of the Celtic people was there when the Romans came. The other branch, the Gaels, lived in Ireland and Scotland. It is of these Gaelic Celts that these stories tell.

The Gaels valued above everything else beauty of person and courage in battle. Their poems and sagas constantly celebrate these virtues. They were a tall race, fair haired or red haired, with white skin and blue or green eyes. A Gaelic warrior wore a smock to his knees that was belted in the middle, which made the smock look like the kilt the Scottish people wear today. Around his neck he wore a torc which was a type of gold necklace, exquisitely decorated and shaped to fit the warrior who wore it. The Gaelic warriors used chariots and went to battle against one another in them.

The palaces of their kings were magnificent. King Conor of Ulster had three houses in his Palace: the Royal Household, the Speckled Household and House of The Red Branch. In the Royal House, there were one hundred and fifty rooms. The walls were made of red yew with copper rivets. The king's own room had bronze walls and a silver ceiling, on which were carved golden birds with eyes of shining diamonds. A silver rod with three golden apples on it lay always at Conor's feet.

7

Whenever he struck this rod, all would be silent.

This Court of King Conor was at Eamhain Macha in Ulster. At the Court, there were many lawyers and priests. A priest in ancient Ireland was called a druid. Above all, there were poets, and it is as well for us that there were, because it was the poets who celebrated the deeds of the heroes. And it is because of this that we are able to know today how the men of Ireland in those times behaved and of the marvellous feats they performed.

There were other kings in Ireland besides Conor. There were kings of the Provinces of Munster and Connaught too. But it was in Conor's kingdom that the most famous warriors of all Ireland lived, the Knights of the Red Branch, and it is of them that I am going to tell in the first part of this book.

CUCHULAIN AND THE KNIGHTS OF THE RED BRANCH

The Red Branch were a band of warrior princes who dedicated themselves to the defence of Ulster against her enemies. There was Conall Cearnach the Victorious. There was Owen, son of Doortact. There was Fergus, Naoise, Ainle and Ardan. Twelve in all there were of the heroes of the Red Branch. But the most famous of them all was Cuchulain, the son of Sualtaim.

First, you must hear of his birth. The Gaels believed that the gods loved men and guided them; and among the Gaels, truth and justice and courage were valued just as they have been in the centuries after Christ. Like Ulysses, the hero of the Greeks, or Siegfried, the German hero, Cuchulain the hero of the Gaels was a favourite of the Gods. Indeed it is said that his father came from the Land Under the Wave, the magic region of the Sidhe or fairies.

Cuchulain's mother was a sister of King Conor of Ulster. Her name was Dechtire. Shortly before her

9

marriage with Sualtaim, she was drinking one day a glass of wine when a mayfly landed in it. She drank the wine and went to sleep with her fifty hand-maidens around her. But the God Lu came to her in her sleep and said:

> 'It was I was the Mayfly that came to you in the glass. You must now come with me to Fairyland, and your fifty maidens with you.'

Dechtire and her maidens were transformed into beautiful birds and they flew to one of the places of the fairies near the River Boyne in County Meath.

King Conor was very disturbed when he found that his sister was gone. Sualtaim, now her husband, was in despair. After many months marching, Conor and Sualtaim arrived on the frontiers of Fairyland and learned that Dechtire was there. They argued with her to come back to them and in the end she agreed.

She brought with her the small son who had been born to her meanwhile, and she and Sualtaim went to live on the plain of Muirthemne. They called the child Setanta.

When the child was about seven, he overheard his parents talking about Eamhain Macha and about the warrior deeds, and the music and the great feats that took place there. He conceived a great ambition to go to Eamhain Macha and play there with the sons of the noblemen and princes who were learning warrior feats and games against the time when they would be men themselves. But his mother thought he was too young to go. The boy was not to be put off, however, and he set out across Slieve Fuad towards Eamhain Macha, bringing with him nothing but his hurling stick and little silver ball.

As Setanta marched across the countryside towards Eamhain Macha, he drove the silver ball in front of him and ran to catch up with it. By this means, the time passed until he arrived at the outskirts of the king's court.

10

Shortly before her marriage with Sualtaim, Dechtire was drinking one day a glass of wine when a mayfly landed in it. She drank the wine and went to sleep with her fifty hand-maidens around her.

11

The first thing he saw there was the young boys of the court playing hurling on the lawn. They were much older than Setanta, but this did not stop him from becoming excited and jumping in amongst them. In a minute, he had the ball between his feet and he drove it through the best of them till he sent it to the goal. The other boys were furious:

> 'Who is this brat who dares to challenge us in this way?' one of the players, Folamh, the son of Conor said. 'He has not asked our permission. Besides, he may be the son of a common person and not entitled to play with noblemen.'

Fergus, one of the Red Branch Knights, happened to be passing and he brought the boy to Conor who was playing chess. Conor asked:

> 'Why did you go in without the permission of the other boys?'
>
> 'I came as a stranger and they did not give me a stranger's hospitality,' the young boy replied proudly.

For he knew that among the Gaels the laws of hospitality were held in high regard. Then Conor asked him who he was, and when he told him he was the son of Dechtire and Sualtaim, the king knew that he was speaking to his own nephew. There was great joy and celebration among the Court and the boys on the hurling field were instructed to let Setanta play with them. But still his strength and skill were so superior that he hurled them right and left and would have continued to do so only that they agreed to treat him not as a small boy but as a young warrior and the equal of them all.

> Thus Setanta grew up in the court of the King of Ulster, and there was not a warrior among that famous band who did not at one time or another instruct him in hero feats.

12

How Cuchulain Got His Name

There was a famous blacksmith in Ulster at that time named Cualann. Blacksmiths were very important people in those days because they forged the weapons with which the warriors fought and protected themselves, and they shod the horses, without which it would have been impossible to move about.

Cualann gave a feast and invited Conor and his court. Conor accepted the invitation and left a message with the boy troop who were out playing games, that Setanta was to follow after when he had finished his exercise. When Conor reached Cualann's house, a great feast was laid before him. There was poetry and song and juggling and recitals, and everybody was merry. Cualann asked the king:

'Will anyone else come after you tonight, Conor?'

Conor, who had drunk a little bit too much and had forgotten about the little boy he had asked to follow him, replied:

'No, there is no one else. Why do you ask?'

'I have,' said Cualann, 'a great hound and I will take the chain off him and he will guard the house. He has great fierceness and the strength of a hundred men.'

'Loose him then,' said Conor, 'and he will guard the house.'

Meanwhile, Setanta had left the boy troop at Eamhain Macha and was proceeding towards the smith's house. When he came to the lawn before Cualann's house, the dog heard him and set up a howl you could hear throughout Ireland. He ran at the little fellow to gobble him in one gulp. The boy took one look at the dog. His stick and ball were the only weapons he had. He straight away drove the hurling ball through the dog's mouth and down his body. When he saw the hound was weakened by this, he took him by the hind legs and killed him.

King Conor, who was inside, heard the noise and jumped up.

'It is surely my sister's son,' he said. 'I had forgotten that I asked him to come here.'

But when Fergus went out and found the little boy safe and sound and carried him inside in his arms, there was great rejoicing. But the smith was sad:

'Ah, you have taken from me,' he said, 'my hound whom I loved and who protected my flocks and herds and all that I had.'

The little boy replied nobly:

'I will make it up to you for what I have done, Cualann. If there is a hound in all Ireland the equal of yours, I will fetch him. If not, I myself will be your watchdog to guard your goods and herds.'

The King and the other noblemen present smiled in satisfaction at the little boy, for this was a manly answer.

Cafad, the druid, said:

'From this day out your name will be Cuchulain, "The Hound of the Smith".'

(Cu in the Irish language means Hound, and Cualann means Smith.) But young Cuchulain would have none of this.

'I am better pleased,' he said, 'with Setanta, son of Sualtaim, for my name.'

'No, take Cuchulain,' said the druid, 'for one day this name will be famous on men's mouths.'

14

The boy took one look at him. His stick and ball were the only weapons he had. He straight away drove the hurling ball through the dog's mouth and down his body. When he saw the hound was weakened by this, he took him by the hind legs and killed him.

15

This pleased the little lad and he accepted the name of Cuchulain from that time on. It was strange in one so young that he should always be concerned with his fame. But this was so with him. One day among the boy troop, asked to perform a feat of arms which could shorten his life, he retorted smartly to the druids around who had dared him to do the deed:

> 'I care not that I live but one night and one day if my deeds will be remembered forever.'

And so it was.

Cuchulain's Manhood and the Cattle Raid of Cooley

When Cuchulain grew to be a man, he was the most famous of all the warriors of the Red Branch. All the women of Ulster loved him for his skill in feats, for the lightness of his leap, for the weight of his wisdom, for the sweetness of his speech, for the comeliness of his looks, for all his gifts. He had the gift of caution in fighting until such time as his anger would come on him and the hero light would shine upon his head. This hero light was from the gods; it was a sign that he had their protection. He had the gift of feats, the gift of chess playing, the gift of draughts playing, the gift of counting, the gift of divining, the gift of right judgement, the gift of beauty. And all the faults they could find in him were three; that he was too young and smoothfaced, so that young men who did not know him would be laughing at him, that he was too daring, and that he was too beautiful.

Whenever Ulster was threatened by her enemies, Cuchulain rushed to the border and there, single-handed, he would hold back hundreds of his enemies.

There were many deeds that Cuchulain became famous for, not only in Ireland, but in Scotland too where he went with his companions to learn warrior feats from Scatach, one of the great woman warriors of the western world. It was after he came back from Scatach that he married Emer, daughter of Fergol Manach the Wily. Then he was given the headship of the young men of Ulster, of the warriors, the poets, the trumpeters, the musicians.

And he brought Emer into the house of the Red Branch and Conor and all the chief men of Ulster gave her a great welcome.

The battle that Cuchulain was to become most famous for, was that of the cattle raid of Cooley. Queen Maeve of Connaught wanted possession of a bull that was owned by an Ulsterman, Daire. Because she could not get it, she sent her battalions across the border into Ulster to fetch the bull. Cuchulain stood alone in the gap, because there was an enchantment over the rest of the men of Ulster. Each night warriors were selected by Maeve and her generals to challenge Cuchulain so that the Connaught men could proceed into Ulster. But he beat each one of them; in one terrible encounter he fought his foster-brother and best friend, Ferdia, who had become chief warrior of Maeve's army and who was sent by the queen to fight Cuchulain. Cuchulain was forced to kill him after they had fought for three days. Each night after battle, they laid aside their arms and salved each other's wounds before retiring to their tent to sleep with their arms around one another.

Etarconal and Natchantar were other warriors who were sent to fight Cuchulain, but lost their lives by his hand.

And now I will tell of how Cuchulain fought Conlaech of Scotland. One day when Cuchulain had grown up and had become a hardened warrior, he and Conor were talking on the lawn outside the palace at

*Queen Maeve of Connaught wanted possession of a bull that was
owned by an Ulsterman, Daire. Because she could not get it,
she sent battalions across the border into Ulster to fetch the bull.*

Eamhain Macha. Conor was getting old and was worried that he had left no son behind him. Because he was a little jealous, he chided Cuchulain with having no son. But Cuchulain laughed scornfully at this and reminded the king that he would leave his name upon the harp and fulfill his old boast: 'Short Life and Long Fame.' Because he was getting old and nervous of his power, Conor decided that he would put Cuchulain under *geasa*. This meant that Cuchulain would have to swear to do whatever the king asked him, no matter how distasteful the deed he was asked to do. Cuchulain was reluctant to do this, but in the end, because he respected Conor and because Conor was old, and because the priests at the court convinced him that it was the wish of the gods that he should take the oath, he did so.

Some time after, news came to the court that a young warrior from Scotland had landed on the coast of Ulster. The warrior refused to give his name. He said he had come from the court of Aoife, Queen of Scotland. Cuchulain had once known Aoife when he lived in Scotland. She had been in love with him before he went back to Ireland to marry Emer. Conall Cearnach the Victorious was sent to question the young man as it was against the code of Ulster for a man to refuse to reveal his name. But the young man still refused, saying that Aoife had given him three commands:

Not to refuse a challenge.
Not to turn back on account of fear.
Not to tell his name on any account.

So, Conall challenged him to combat, and extraordinary as it is to relate, the young man bested Conall, though he did not kill him. Conall went back, crestfallen, to Eamhain Macha and told the king what had happened.

'This is indeed an extraordinary youth who can best Conall,' said Conor. 'Who shall be sent against this man?'

Strangely, Cuchulain held himself aloof, sulking in the background. There had been something about the appearance of the youth that had affected him in a curious way. Conor singled Cuchulain out, however, from the others and ordered him to proceed to the coast and fight Aoife's warrior. A croaking noise from the druids in the background reminded Cuchulain that he was under *geasa*. In the end, he gave in and set out with a heavy heart, for somehow he did not want to do battle with this young warrior from Scotland.

It was a hard fight; seldom was such a battle seen. The men of Ulster wondered that the young man could stand so well against Cuchulain. Though Cuchulain was the champion of Ireland and Scotland, he was hard pressed by the daring of this young man. His anger grew that he could not subdue him. And the hero light, the sign that Cuchulain was beloved by the gods, and which they had given him for his protection, began to shine about his head. When Aoife's warrior saw the flame, he was stricken with horror. He was the son of Aoife, and she had told him that his own unknown father was born of the gods and that the sign of his divine birth was that a hero light played at times over his head. He knew then that it was his own father he was fighting. So, as he cast his spear, he swerved it to the left, deliberately missing Cuchulain, for he was unwilling to slay his father. When the spear missed him, Cuchulain saw his chance. He leaped in and with a mighty blow drove his spear through the heart of the young man, wounding him mortally.

'Tell me your name,' said Cuchulain, standing over the dying youth.

Tears came into the young man's eyes, and they were not from anger but from sadness.

'My name is Conlaech,' he said. 'I am your son, Cuchulain, son of the greatest warrior in Erin, the

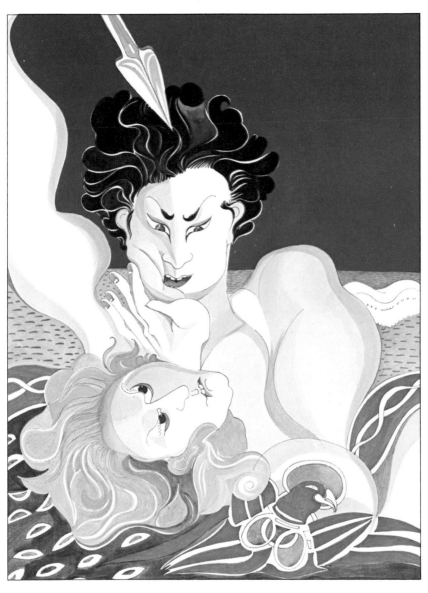

When the spear missed him, Cuchulain saw his chance. He leaped in and with a mighty blow drove his spear through the heart of the young man, wounding him mortally.

Then Cuchulain roared and made great bellows of anger over
the body of his son. After a while, he rose and rushed down
towards Bailes Strand, swearing that the gods had played him a
trick by making him kill his own son.

Hound of Ulster. My mother pledged me to secrecy that I should not say who I am.'

'A curse upon your mother for her treachery,' said Cuchulain. 'It is through her evil thoughts that these tears have been brought on us.'

'A curse upon my mother too,' said the dying Conlaech, 'for it is she who put me under oath not to say who I was.'

And the sorrow of death came on Conlaech, and Cuchulain took a sword and put it through him sooner than leave his son in the pain and agony he was in.

Then Cuchulain wandered through the ranks of the soldiers of Eamhain and made a great lament:

'I am the father that killed his son, the fine green branch there is no hand to help or shelter.

'Oh, if my son were alive, my fair son, my only son, the men of Ireland from sea to sea would not be equal to his strength.

'It is well for the house of the Red Branch that it was not they who killed my son.

'I am a raven that has no home: I am a boat going from wave to wave; I am a ship that has lost its rudder; I am the apple left on the tree; it is little I thought of falling from it; grief and sorrow will be with me from this time.'

Then Cuchulain roared and made great bellows of anger over the body of his son. After a while, he rose and rushed down towards Bailes Strand, swearing that the gods had played him a trick by making him kill his own son. Wildly he shouted to the sky, with the wind running through his hair and the salt sea beating on his face. He waved his sword defiantly towards the sky challenging the gods. Then he turned and ran towards the waves shouting that he would die fighting them.

The Death of Cuchulain

Some say that Cuchulain died challenging the gods and fighting the waves at Bailes Strand. But that is not true. What actually happened was this. There were many in Ireland at that time who harboured great envy of Cuchulain. Daire, King of Munster; Lu, whose father Corrig had been slain by Cuchulain; Erc, the son of Carberry, High King of Ros na Ree, who also met his death by Cuchulain's hand, and others.

Above all, Queen Maeve of Connaught hated him. She sent her emissary to Lu and Daire and others, and by skilful means roused them so that they could think of nothing else except to make an end to the Ulsterman. They gathered their armies together and proceeded north, their only purpose being to engage the Red Branch in battle and in the course of this to kill Cuchulain. Up in Ulster, King Conor heard that the regiments of the men of Ireland were proceeding north. He sent a message to Cuchulain at Dundalk where he was living at that time and asked him to move north to Ulster where he would be safe with the Knights of the Red Branch. When Cuchulain had come to Eamhain Macha, they left him there with Niamh. She loved him so dearly that they knew she would not let him out to battle with the Connaught men, no matter how much he longed for the affray. But a daughter of Coltain, whose father had fallen by Cuchulain's hand, using a magic spell adopted the form of Niamh. Thus transformed, she induced Cuchulain to put on his armour and face the enemy on the boundaries of Ulster. When the battalions of Lu and Erc saw Cuchulain, they were pleased indeed, for it was with this end, that they might take him and kill him in battle, that they had come to Ulster.

Cuchulain was not at this time the warrior he had been. Age was beginning to chain his limbs. Nevertheless, he bid the men of Connaught come against him and he

Then they saw a raven settle on his shoulder and drink his blood: 'It is not on that pillar birds were used to settle,' said Erc.

did his three thunder feats and drove through them in his chariot, scattering thousands through the fields which were red with blood. But though he performed wondrous deeds, Cuchulain's enemies saw that age had weakened his endurance. Laeg, Cuchulain's chariot driver, was killed by Lu. Cuchulain was not dismayed, however:

> 'I will be a fighter chariot driver as well today,' he said.

Then they slew his horse, the horse that Cuchulain loved, the Grey of Macha. Finally, Lu cast a spear that made a great wound in Cuchulain. As he lay on the ground, he asked his enemies if he might go to a lake to drink because he was thirsty. In the warrior tradition, they let him go, provided he promised to come back. But when Cuchulain reached the lake, he was unable to walk back; so.he drank some water, washed himself and bid his enemies come and get him.

There was a stone pillar by the lake. Cuchulain crawled to it, and, with his breast belt, tied himself to the pillar so that he might die standing up. He felt it unworthy that a Knight of the Red Branch should meet his death lying down.

But so great was the fame and reputation of Cuchulain that the men of Connaught feared to approach him while he was still alive. Strapped to a pillar in the setting sun, he stood facing them, his head drooped on his shoulder.

Then they saw a raven settle on his shoulder and drink his blood:

> 'It is not on that pillar birds were used to settle,' said Erc.

Then they knew he was dead.

Thus it was that the great Cuchulain, son of Sualtaim, was slain.

THE FATE OF THE CHILDREN OF LIR

Before the Gaels came to Ireland, the Tuatha de Danaan were kings there. They were tall and fair like the Gaels who conquered them; some knowledgeable scholars are of the opinion that the Tuatha de Danaan were the same people who now live in Denmark. This may be true, for there are many people in Ireland with the appearance of Swedes, Danes and Norwegians.

However it may be, after they were conquered by the Gaels, the Tuatha de Danaan went to live on their own in another part of Ireland. There they elected a king, Bov Deareg. His rival for the throne was Lir. When Lir lost the kingship, he went to live apart from the rest of the Tuatha de Danaan. Later he married Aev, one of three foster children of Bov Deareg. She bore Lir four children, three boys, Fiachra, Aodh and Conn, and one daughter, Fionnuala.

Shortly after the birth of Conn, Aev died; and because he needed a mother for his children, Lir married Aev's sister Aoife. The children were the most beautiful ever seen in Ireland. They had bright red lips, snow white skin, and eyes that were green when they gazed upon the sea, blue when they looked at the sky. So handsome were they that King Bov Deareg himself used to come over just to look at them in joy and delight.

This made Aoife madly jealous. One day, she yoked a chariot and put the four children in it and set out for Bov Deareg's palace. On the way, they stopped at the Lake of the Oaks, and she sent the children in for a bathe. While they were in the water, she touched them with a magic wand, and they were turned into four swans.

'It is with flocks of birds now your cries will be heard forever,' she cried triumphantly to the four children.

The children were terrified to have this magic trick played on them; and they begged her to undo her magic and give them back their human forms. She would not. Finally, Fionnuala, who was the eldest of the four and the wisest said:

'You have done a wicked thing on us, but at least will you not put some boundary to the enchant-ment, so that one day we will be human beings again?'

'I will,' said Aoife. 'But it would be better for you if you had not asked me. For three hundred years, you will remain on the Lake of the Oaks: for three hundred years after you will go to the Isle of Maoile, between Ireland and Scotland; and for three hundred years more you will remain at Innis Gluaire, on the wild North Coast of Ireland. You will not get human form again until on this Lake you will hear a bell chiming in honour of God, three times each day.'

With that, her face hardened and she ordered her step-children out of her sight. But as she turned away, her heart was touched for a second, and she said to the four swan children:

'You may keep your own human voices and sing the sweet music of the fairies. And your own sense

28

*While they were in the water, she touched them with a magic
wand, and they were turned into four swans, white and beautiful.
'It is with flocks of birds now your cries will be heard forever,'
she cried.*

of nobility will stay with you, that way it will not weigh so heavy on you to be in the shape of birds.'

When Lir heard of the fate of his children, he rushed to the side of the lake. He saw the four swans and asked them what had happened. Fionnuala told him what Aoife had done.

'We have not the power,' said Fionnuala, 'to live with any person at all from this time; but we have our own language, the Irish, and we have the power to sing sweet music, and it is enough to satisfy the whole race of men to be listening to that music. Let you stop here tonight,' she said, 'and we will be making music for you.'

Lir waited with his retinue that night by the lake and they were delighted with the music they heard. Then he went in anger to King Bov Deareg and told him what Aoife had done. And the king struck Aoife with the druid wand and she turned into a witch of the air and she went away in that shape, and she is in it yet.

Meanwhile on the lake, there gathered each day thousands of the nobles and peoples of Ireland to listen to the wonderful music of the swan children. There never was any music or any delight heard in Ireland compared with that music of the swans. And they used to be telling stories, to be talking with the men of Ireland every day and with their teachers and their fellow-pupils and their friends. And every night they used to sing the sweet music of the fairies, and everyone that heard that music would sleep soundly and quiet, whatever trouble or long sickness might be on him; for everyone that heard the music of the birds, it is happy and contented he would be after it.

At the end of three hundred years on the lake, Fionnuala said:

'Now we must leave the Lake of the Oaks and go to the Isle of Maoile.'

30

And the king struck Aoife with the druid wand and she turned
into a witch of the air and she went away in that shape, and
she is in it yet; and will be in it until the end of life and time.

Her brothers were sad when they heard this, because in their own way they had been happy on the Lake of the Oaks, talking and singing with the Gaels and the Tuatha de Danaan.

They took flight to Maoile, and it was three hundred years they spent on that island. Often their feathers were frozen from the ice and their wings were heavy and wet from the cold sea spray. There was one time in a furious storm the children of Lir almost lost one another. What would have happened to them then? They were neither swans nor human beings, and had they been apart from one another, who in the world could they have turned to for companionship? A fierce burst of wind tore them apart. As they were swept away from one another, Fionnuala, who was the wisest of the four, shouted that they should meet again on the island of Seals. After three days being buffeted around by the winds and the sea, Fionnuala reached the island of Seals where she waited for her brothers to turn up. She waited two days and there was no sign of them. Now she was sad because she felt she might not see her brothers again. But there against the setting sun was Conn, the youngest of her brothers, flying towards her, his head hanging and feathers wet through, and after him presently came Fiachra, wet and perished with the cold. She spread both of them under her wings to dry, and they lay there on the Seal island, the three swan children waiting for their brother to come. At last he came, too, with his feathers beautiful, because he had been flying in a region where there was sun and comfort. On that lonely island in the Irish sea, the four swan children made music and sang songs together. And it is a great pity there was no one to hear them except the seals on that cruel island.

It is little chance they had of singing or making music or telling tales in the next hundred years. For the sound of the wind drowned their music, and they were too cold by far on that awful island of Maoile to tell tales to

32

On that lonely island in the Irish sea, the four swan children made
music and sang songs together. And it is a great pity there was no
one to hear them except the seals on that cruel island.

one another. Three hundred years they spent on the island of Maoile, and then three hundred more on Innis Gluaire. And finally they decided that they could return to their own country of Lir. So they set off one day, flying along and singing songs the while. But when they returned, there was no one left of all those they had known in their lifetime. The castle was empty and nothing in it but green hillocks and thickets of nettles. Neither was there a fire or a hearthstone. They stopped near the ruins of their own home that night. Next day they went back to Innis Gluaire and all the birds of the country gathered near them on Loc na n-Ean, the lake of the birds. And they used to go out to feed everyday to the far parts of the country and to all the western islands of Connaught.

About this time in history, St Patrick arrived in Ireland, to convert the Irish to Christianity. His missionaries and priests travelled all over Ireland. One of them, St Mackevig, came to Innis Gluaire. On the island, he built a little chapel. One day he was putting on his vestments to say mass when he heard the song of the swan children coming across the water to him:

> 'That is most beautiful music,' he said to himself. 'I must go and find it, because people who sing as beautifully as this could be singing hymns in my church to the praise of God.'

He went out and searched around. After some time when he had questioned many people as to the source of the music, he discovered to his astonishment that the music came not from human beings, but from four swans. St Mackevig was a very kind man and his heart was touched with the predicament of the children of Lir who were neither swans nor human. He asked them would they come to his church each day, because he thought they might take comfort from the mass and the praises that were offered to God. They told him they would come, and before he left, he made them a little chain of silver,

34

one between Fionnuala and Conn, and another between Aodh and Fiachra.

They arrived along at his church next morning. There was quite a lot of trouble about this, as the holy men from other islands near Innis Gluaire heard about it, and they said it was not right to bring swans into Holy Mass. The people of Innis Gluaire too said that it was not right to let swans into church. But St Mackevig was not only a saint, he was a holy man as well; and since, from time to time, he had quite intimate conversations with God, he was perfectly certain that the Almighty would be very pleased with the beautiful music which would come from the side of the altar when the children of Lir would sing there.

So it happened, at Mass one morning in Innis Gluaire, that the children of Lir were beside the priest on the altar. Three bells were rung for the Elevation of the Host when an astonishing thing happened. The feathers fell from the bodies of the children of Lir and in half a second they had got back their human forms again. This was the prophecy of their step-mother; that her curse would go from them when they would hear a bell rung in Ireland three times each day in honour of God.

But now we come to the saddest part of the story. What St Mackevig and the other people at Mass saw was not three handsome young men and a fair young girl, but one lean old woman and three withered men. For it was nine hundred years since the curse was put on them. St Mackevig was touched at this sad sight:

> 'It is a pity for you, O Children of Lir, to become human beings again, and at the end of all to find yourselves like this.'

He hurried away for a few minutes and came back with the Holy Water. He gave them God's blessing and baptized them. Shortly afterwards they died. Their time on earth was a sad one. It would not be so in eternity.

Three bells were rung for the Elevation of the Host when an astonishing thing happened. The feathers fell from the bodies of the children of Lir and in half a second they had got back their human forms again.

DEIRDRE AND THE SONS OF USNA

This is one of the most famous love stories of all Europe. It precedes the tale of Tristan and Iseult and the Knights of the Round Table by many thousands of years.

This Irish hero tale tells how a beautiful women, Deirdre, was the cause of the death of a famous family of brothers, the sons of Usna, and how her beauty drove the King of Ulster to do deeds so treacherous that, for centuries afterwards when the men of Ireland spoke of betrayal, they always placed this monarch first in the list of traitors.

This beautiful girl Deirdre was born in Ulster. The King of Ulster at that time was Conor MacNessa. He ruled over Cuchulain and the Red Branch Knights of whom we have read in other pages.

On the day when Deirdre was born, there was a fearful storm and most of Ulster was covered in flood. King Conor had gone to visit Felim, the son of Dall, his favourite storyteller. Felim had prepared a magnificent feast for the king and the Knights of the Red Branch. They did not mind the rain too much for they were safe in Felim's castle eating and drinking, warmed by enormous fires, and singing songs and playing the harp.

Half way through the feast, it was learned that a

daughter had been born to Felim. Conor sent Caffa, his druid, to see the new-born child and ordered him to come back and tell him what he had seen. About an hour later, Conor noticed Caffa standing white-faced at the door.

'What's wrong with you,' said Conor. 'Come in, please. Is the child dead?'

'No,' said Caffa. 'She is the most beautiful child ever born in Ireland. She will grow up to have raven black hair, whose sheen will blind those who look at it without masking their eyes, her own eyes will be green and her lips the colour of the Christmas berry.'

'Then, why,' said Conor, 'do you look as if you had seen one of those spirits that you call down to frighten us when we are not obeying the will of the gods?'

'Because, O King,' said Caffa, 'I have looked into the future and it has been told to me that Deirdre will bring trouble and sorrow to the men of Ulster and that there will be blood spilt because of her beauty and that brother will be torn from brother.'

Conor was in good humour with the drink and food and the amusing talk, and he was not to be put off by the druid's gloomy prophecies. But he knew enough about priest craft to know that there might be something in what was said. So to put everybody's mind at ease, he stood up and announced:

'When this child grows up, I will be her guardian. When she is of age, I will marry her. In this way there will be no dispute among the men of Ireland over Deirdre for I am king. Let her be taken from her parents and put into the hands of Lavarcham who has nursed my family. She will bring up Deirdre and every day she will come to me and tell me how the child is progressing and whether she is going to be beautiful as these magicians tell me she will be.'

But, because the druid had power to see into the future, he was still sad. For he knew that nothing the king would do could upset the plan ordained by fate, and that some day Deirdre would bring sorrow to the Gaels. He

'She is the most beautiful child ever born in Ireland. She will grow up to have raven black hair, whose sheen will blind those who look at it without masking their eyes, her own eyes will be green and her lips the colour of the Christmas berry.'

39

was right. Because to this day in Ireland that child is remembered as Deirdre of the Sorrows.

Deirdre grew to womanhood as had been foretold. Indeed she was so beautiful that Conor was very nervous of letting her move among the young men of his court. He ordered her nurse to keep her as much as possible in the castle that he had built for her on the edge of Eamhain Macha.

Deirdre's nurse, Lavarcham, was very fond of her. Often she wished to bring the girl out among the other young people who played around about the court but she was afraid because she had strict instructions from the king not to do so.

After all, Conor was getting old and he was afraid that, if Deirdre had too many young men she would choose them instead of him who had sworn in front of the court that he would marry her.

One day Deirdre said to Lavarcham, 'I had a dream last night. I dreamt that I had a great bowl of gold and honey in front of me...and then a jug of thick rich cream was poured into it, making a hole in the honey. When I looked at it, I thought of a young man whom I had seen years ago when you brought me to watch the boy warriors of the Red Branch playing their games and practising their feats in the field. His hair was the colour of honey and his skin was as white as cream. Can you remember him, Lavarcham?'

Lavarcham told her that it was probably of Naisi she was thinking, one of three boys who had become famous warriors and who were now known the length and breadth of Ulster for their skill and sword play, for their strength in leaping and jumping, for bravery and chariot-racing, and their complete lack of fear in battle. They were called the sons of Usna and their names were Naisi, Ardan and Ainle.

Deirdre decided to try a trick in order to meet Naisi. She wheedled Lavarcham into getting her

'I had a dream last night. I dreamt that I had a great bowl of gold and honey in front of me . . . and then a jug of thick rich cream was poured into it, making a hole in the honey.'

permission from Conor to walk to the woods and mountains near the court. Because she was a young girl, she believed that things would somehow turn out her way and, though there was not really very much chance of her meeting Naisi in the hills, Deirdre nevertheless believed that if she went there often enough fate would bring her in contact with Naisi.

So it turned out.

One day walking along a forest path, she saw coming towards her a man the like of which she had never seen before or even imagined in the many dreams she had had about Naisi.

There they were in front of her, running along a forest path, the sons of Usna, and in the middle of them was Naisi.

When they saw her they stopped. Ainle first, and then Ardan, came up and gave her a kiss of welcome. Then her heart nearly burst and her face lit with joy as she beheld Naisi in front of her; it was the same young man she had seen playing in the fields of Eamhain Macha when she was a girl and he was a boy. He had eyes like a blue sky seen through smoke rising from the fire, his hair was gold, and his cheeks white, and his lips red like a girl's. He was tall and lithe and he walked with the poise and power of a leopard until he ran when he was like a deer skipping through the forest, graceful and carefree.

Deirdre knew then that some day she would marry him. Naisi was puzzled at first by the whole affair. But after he had met her a few times in the forest, it came to him like a dream that he too would marry Deirdre.

So he and his brothers took her away from Lavarcham and they went to live in the mountains.

When Conor heard about this, he was furious. In the first place, he had looked forward to marrying Deirdre whom he had brought up since she was a child. Secondly, he did not like losing her to the sons of Usna who were his warriors. Thirdly, he did not like the fact that, because they were in the mountains, he could no longer avail himself of the services of Naisi, Ardan and Ainle as Knights of the Red Branch. An appalling enmity sprang up between him and the sons of Usna.

In the end it became so bad that Naisi decided to emigrate to Scotland which was at that time called Alba. The sons of Usna had been in Scotland a number of times and in fact owned a considerable kingdom there as a result of battles they had fought. So it was not hard for Naisi and his brothers to go there.

Yet it is said by those who tell the story of the sons of Usna that there was never a day while they were living in Scotland that Naisi, Ardan and Ainle were not lonely for Ireland, though they knew it was impossible to go back there because of the wrath of the King of Ulster.

Exile in Scotland

In Scotland, the sons of Usna and Deirdre lived at the head of a lake called Etive. They caught glittering salmon in the lakes and rivers and brought them home in the evening to Deirdre. They hunted deer among the green hills of Scotland, catching them with astonishing skill, for the sons of Usna were known all over Scotland and Ireland for fleetness of foot and deftness in hunting. In the evening, they would bring the spoils of the hunt in to Deirdre and she would have a marvellous meal laid out which the sons of Usna would eat sitting around the fire, telling stories, laughing and singing, just as they had done in the years when they had lived in Ireland.

None of the brothers was jealous of Naisi and Deirdre. The sons of Usna were bound together in the most perfect bond of warrior comradeship. No one could break this. Because Naisi loved Deirdre, they respected and supported that love even though it meant living in exile away from the island that had been the centre of their lives until they met Deirdre.

One winter they all roved down to an island that to this day is called Oilean na Rón or the Island of Seals. There they built a fortress for Deirdre and from this place they set out to conquer Scotland. It was not difficult for the sons of Usna to do this as there were few warriors in the western world that could equal them. Soon they had become monarchs of a large part of western Scotland.

One day Deirdre and Naisi were playing chess. In between the moves she was watching his handsome face, lost in thought, set against the blue Scottish lakes and misty hills. Suddenly she realized she had won the game and laughed a little in triumph.

Naisi looked up at her and there was a sudden bitterness in his eyes. 'What matter if one game is lost,' he said, 'if all else is lost?' This was the first indication Deirdre had had of how much his exile from Ireland had hurt Naisi and his brothers.

While they were playing a second game of chess, a cry came echoing up from the glens below. Hearing it, Naisi cried, 'By God, this is the voice of a son of Ireland.'

Deirdre heard it too, but she pretended not to recognize it as an Irish voice. A sudden fear gripped her heart. She did not want Naisi to have anything to do with Ireland because she was afraid of the consequences of returning there and of the anger of Conor. So she said, 'Naisi, that's the voice of a man of Scotland returning from a hunt.'

'No, it's not,' said Naisi, as he heard the shout once more. 'That's the voice of a man from the country I love and which is closest to my heart.' He jumped up from the game of chess upsetting the board and started to run down the glen, rushing wildly through the grass and over the stones until he found the man who was making the shouts.

While they were playing a second game of chess, a cry came echoing up from the glens below. Hearing it, Naisi cried, 'By God, this is the voice of a son of Ireland.'

As the boat drew away from the shores of Scotland Deirdre sang a farewell which has been handed down among the people of Ireland even to this day.

It was Fergus MacRoy, one of the warriors of the Red Branch who had been sent by King Conor to try and persuade the sons of Usna to come back to Ireland with Deirdre. Actually Fergus MacRoy had come in good faith because be had been a close friend of Naisi and his brothers. He did not know that Conor had sent him over to get the exiles home only so that he could imprison the sons of Usna and win Deirdre for his wife.

The king had given him his word, that no harm would come to Naisi, Ainle and Ardan, and it had never been known that the head of the Knights of the Red Branch, which Conor was, would break a promise given in warrior bond.

Naisi and his brothers were overjoyed when they heard the news that they now could go back to Ireland, the country which they loved, with welcome. They could return with Deirdre for whose sake they had left.

The night before they left Scotland, Deirdre had a dream in which she saw a raven flying towards her bearing the three leaves of a yew tree. She interpreted this to mean, for the yew tree is a symbol of death, that the sons of Usna would die, hurled into eternity by Conor just as the leaves had been blown off the yew tree in the dream by the wind of death.

But next morning, Naisi and the other brothers only laughed at her dream, so happy were they to be going back to Ulster.

Apart from her fear, Deirdre was unhappy at leaving Scotland anyway. She had grown to love the country in the years that she was there. And remember, of course, that she was the centre of a wonderful band of brothers famous throughout the two islands at that time for their generosity and gaiety. As the boat drew away from the shores of Scotland, Deirdre sang a farewell which has been handed down among the people of Ireland even to this day:

'Farewell, dear Alba of the free.'

The Death of Naisi and Deirdre

While the returned exiles were feasting, Conor sent Lavarcham along to meet the group and find out how Deirdre was. When Lavarcham beheld the child she had reared, the tears ran down her cheeks. She knew in her heart of hearts that trouble would come to Deirdre and Naisi and this filled her with sadness for, after Deirdre, more than anyone else in the world, she loved Naisi.

Deirdre told Lavarcham of her dream before she left Scotland and of how she was afraid that Conor would take revenge on Naisi and his brothers. Lavarcham was so horrified when she heard this that she went back to Conor and told him that, while Naisi had become more handsome and virile in exile, little of Deirdre's beauty remained to her. This was so that Conor would lose interest in Deirdre and forget about his revenge on Naisi and his brothers.

Conor, however, was a cunning old brute. He called Trendorn, whose father had been slain in a feud by Naisi, and sent him to spy on the newly-returned group. Naisi was playing chess with Deirdre when he saw Trendorn peeping through a small window. Expertly Naisi let fly a chessman at Trendorn who ran back to Conor with his eye badly injured. Trendorn was naturally in a flaming temper and he told Conor that he had seen Deirdre and she was still the most beautiful woman in Ireland or Scotland.

Conor's desire rose in him now like a flood and he determined to get Deirdre by any means even if it meant breaking his word to the sons of Usna and living on in history as the man who had been unfaithful to his warrior bond. He launched his army against the sons of Usna. When the pursuit reached the Red Branch House, Illan and Buinne went out to defend the sons of Usna as their father Fergus had ordered them to do. They fulfilled their

Conor's desire rose in him now like a flood and he determined to get Deirdre by any means even if it meant breaking his word to the sons of Usna and living on in history as the man who had been unfaithful to his warrior band.

father's command even against their own king. But Conor's treachery was beyond bounds. He tricked Buinne into coming over to his side and, though Illan fought bravely to protect Deirdre and the brothers, the group was very soon surrounded.

Naisi, Ainle and Ardan then had a council of war. They decided they would break out of the Red Branch House and face the hosts of Conor who were closing in. Naisi put Deirdre on his shoulder and together the three brothers faced the enemy.

Incredible as it may seem, so brave and skilful in battle were the sons of Usna that eventually Conor became afraid that these three men would destroy his own army. He called his priests, his druids, and begged them to put an enchantment on Naisi and his brothers.

Then the druids made a spell, so that the sons of Usna were suddenly confronted by a thick forest. Undaunted, they sped through it, their feet skimming in and out of the trees, looking neither right nor left till they came out at the other end.

'Try another spell,' said Conor, in fury. The druids cast another spell and conjured up a cold, grey sea with harsh waves breaking across it. But Naisi stepped into the waves with Deirdre on his shoulders and, followed by his brothers, was not deterred even by this magic ocean.

Now the druids were baffled. They cast another spell and froze the sea into ice so that the sons of Usna had to fight their way through mountains of frozen water which cut their feet and sliced the skin off their hands. Soon it became too much even for these heroic brothers. Naisi leaned against Ardan and he found to his horror that his brother was frozen, and it was like this too with Ainle.

'Lean against me,' said Naisi to his brother, 'and my body will give you heat against this awful cold.'

He took his brothers in his arms so that for a while

50

Naisi leaned against Arden and he found to his horror that his brother was frozen, and it was like this too with Ainle. 'Lean against me,' said Naisi to his brother, 'and my body will give you heat against this awful cold.'

From Deirdre's grave a young pine tree grew and from Naisi's another grew also. After a few years, it could be seen that the branches of one tree were stretching towards the branches of the other and that they would eventually entwine across the lake.

52

they had some comfort from the heat of their brother's body. Naisi sang songs to Ainle and Ardan that they had known since they were boys and it was in this way that the two sons of Usna met their death.

When it dawned on Naisi that his two brothers were dead, he gave in himself and sank down on the ice to die. The druids watched carefully to see how long it would take Naisi to die. They were very careful to make sure that he was dead, for had not he and his two brothers almost conquered the armies of Ulster?

Eventually the spell was lifted and it became possible to see Deirdre standing over the bodies of Naisi, Ardan and Ainle, crying out again and again, and weeping piteously for the dead men.

Conor went up to her and tried to take her away, but she refused to be parted from the bodies.

When they were laid in their grave, she jumped in to Naisi's tomb, and threw her arms around his dead body. Feeling him again beside her and knowing he was dead, her heart broke within her and presently too she lay dead beside him, her lover.

Deirdre and Naisi were buried in one tomb.

Afterwards Conor became angry at the thought of this and had her body taken up and laid at the other side of the lake. From Deirdre's grave, however, a young pine tree grew and, curiously enough, from Naisi's grave on the other side of the lake another pine tree grew also. After a few years, it could be seen that the branches of one tree were stretching towards the branches of the other and that they would eventually entwine across the lake.

Conor would have had the trees cut down but the men of Ulster prevented him.

It happened this way as it was foretold at her birth that Deirdre would bring tribulation to the men of Ulster and that the flower of their chivalry would fall into the hollow earth. To this day, Deirdre is never referred to by any other name but that of Deirdre of the Sorrows.

ST PATRICK

Most people know that it was St Patrick who first converted the Irish people to Christianity in 432, over fifteen hundred years ago. What they do not know is that Ireland's national saint was a Briton! He was born and lived in the west coast of England as the son of a Briton who had accepted the Roman way of life. The Romans at this time had conquered Britain which was ruled from Rome as part of the vast imperial complex that the Romans had imposed on Europe, with the exceptions of the areas ruled by the Celts and the Germans. The Irish had not been conquered by the Romans and Irish kings frequently made raids on Roman Britain in search of slaves.

It was on one of these raids that Patrick was taken prisoner and brought to Ireland. The leader of the expedition that captured Patrick was Niall of the Nine Hostages, one of the most famous kings of Ireland. His name is important because, by a curious twist of fate when Patrick was to come back to Ireland many years later as a missionary, it was from Niall's son that he received his first greeting. Patrick was brought to Antrim in the North of Ireland and was set to work as a herdsman for a landowner named Meliuc. In the harsh winter of that part of Ireland, he lived on Slemish mountain, minding sheep. He must have been a hardy lad for he lasted this out for seven years without any great harm coming to him.

Patrick was brought to Antrim in the North of Ireland and was set to work as a herdsman for a landowner named Meluic. In the harsh winter of that part of Ireland, he lived on Slemish mountain, minding sheep.

At the end of this time, one night as he was saying his prayers (for Patrick had always remained a devout Christian, the religion he had been brought up in), Patrick heard a voice. He took the voice to be the voice of God, telling him to escape from Meliuc, and seek a boat in the southern part of the island which would take him to Britain.

Patrick heeded the voice and decided to escape from Meliuc's service. He made plans, watched his chance and, one cold winter night, crept out of the shed in which he slept and set out for the southern part of the country.

Sure enough, after he had travelled some days, he found a boat near Wexford. This boat was on the point of leaving for Britain. Patrick spoke to the captain and, after some argument, the captain agreed to take the young Briton on board. The boat was bringing a cargo of Irish wolfhounds to Britain; one of the most prized breeds in Europe.

When the crew landed in Britain, they had to transport the dog cages across country. It was then that poor Patrick fell into even more misfortune. He was captured by a band of brigands who were roving England and taken to the Continent once again as a slave.

Patrick wandered for seven years up and down Europe – France, Germany, Italy – trying to find himself and discover what he should make of his life. He had no doubt about what he wanted to do. He studied to be a priest at Lérin Monastery on an island off the beautiful Cote d'Azur.

Then he went back to Britain as an ordained priest to be among his own people. But he was not long in Britain when a strange thing happened. He heard voices in his sleep one night saying to him: 'We beseech thee, holy youth, to come and walk once more amongst us.'

He knew immediately it was the voice of the Irish people and his love for them woke in his breast again.

Oh yes, they had made him a slave. He had spent many months out on the harsh mountains of Antrim because of the cruelty of his Irish employer. But in Ireland, Patrick had grown to love the people. He loved their gaiety, their ways, their poetry, their dancing, their love of nature. He had fallen in love, though he had not realized it until this moment, with the wild, mystical landscape of Ireland and with the way of life of her peoples.

In a dream then, it was revealed to Patrick what his mission in life was to be: he was to convert the Irish to Christianity. He set out to Europe to study once more so that he would be fully equipped intellectually for the task he had set himself.

He settled down at the Monastery of Auxerre in France and there became noted for his zeal in studies and the discipline of his daily life. He had one great disappointment in this period. The monks at Auxerre decided that the time had come to send a mission to Ireland. But despite his secret ambition, Patrick was passed over in the choice of leader of the expedition. He volunteered but for some reason, he was rejected.

And now, instead, another monk, Palladius, was sent to Ireland. Patrick was brokenhearted. After a year or two, however, he learned that Palladius had died and that another mission was to be sent to Ireland.

Patrick was ordered to Rome and in 432, at the age of forty eight, was consecrated Bishop by Pope Celestine.

He had achieved his life's ambition. He was to go back to Ireland where he had lived as a slave and convert the Irish to Christianity.

In the winter of 432, Patrick and twenty five others set sail from France to Ireland. They made a few forays before finally settling on a place to establish their mission.

St Patrick Returns to Ireland

At one spot, in Delvin, County Westmeath, Patrick lay down on the rich, green grass to sleep because the midday sun had grown so hot. A young nobleman, whose father was a local prince, saw Patrick asleep. He could see by the cut of him, that he was a princely person, and so laid some flowers on Patrick's breast as a tribute.

One of Patrick's followers rebuked the young man, saying he would wake the Bishop. Patrick awoke at this and, seeing the flowers and hearing the reproof, said, 'Don't mind, my son, some day you will be my heir.' The young man's name was Benen. Later he was to become Benignus, Patrick's most devoted follower. When Patrick died many years later, it was Benignus he appointed to be his successor as Bishop of Armagh and all Ireland.

Eventually, the group settled down at Slane, County Meath, where Dichiu, a local landowner, sheltered the group and was baptized a Christian.

Patrick wintered at Slane through the kindness of Dichiu and when spring came decided that he would go and confront the High King at Tara. He was warned against this by Dichiu who told him that this part of the year was consecrated to a special pagan rite, the Rite of Spring, and it was no time to confront the king. On March 25 each year, the King of Ireland inaugurated the Festival of Spring by igniting a great fire on the Hill of Tara which was seen for miles around. It was a symbol to the people that the earth gods would renew again the world with the birth of a new season and that the blight which winter brings was over. The king had laid down a law that no fire should be kindled anywhere in Ireland on that date until the great flame leaped up from Tara Hill.

Patrick decided to challenge the king. He directed on the morning of March 25 that a beacon should be lit at Slane. Full of the zeal of their mission, his followers piled

A young nobleman, whose father was a local prince, saw Patrick
asleep. He could see by the cut of him that he was a princely
person, and so laid some flowers on Patrick's breast as a tribute.

fuel on the burning fire till the flames leaped into the sky. Patrick encouraged them vigorously.

At Tara, King Laoghaire, surrounded by noblemen and druids, waited to light the fire. As he was about to do so, he saw flames lighting the sky across the fields. He was livid with anger. This was a direct challenge to his authority. Immediately he called his lawyers and priests and asked them where the fire came from. They told him it had been lit at Slane.

Laoghaire gathered his war chariots together and he and the chief princes of Ireland set out without delay to find who this usurper was who dared challenge the king's right to light the first fire of spring. When they arrived, Patrick was ready for them. It was a curious meeting this. On the one side was the royal heir of an ancient kingdom and his court, attired in colourful costumes with gold ornaments and jewels. On the other, a band of missionaries clad in the Roman fashion, in simple vestments. On his head their leader wore a tall cap rather like a bishop's mitre would look today. The king and his followers wore their hair long and had beards while Patrick and his companions were clean-shaven in the Roman fashion.

As soon as Laoghaire got down off his chariot, Patrick confronted him. Speaking coldly, clearly and precisely, he told the king that he and his group were Christians; that he personally had come back to Ireland where he had been brought first as a slave by Niall, Laoghaire's father, and that, apart from spreading the gospel, he had no other intentions in Ireland.

To the great annoyance of the druids, Laoghaire seemed impressed by Patrick's demeanour and asked him to come and visit the Royal Court at Tara next day.

Next day, an astonishing procession marched out of Slane. It was led by Patrick, carrying a great cross, followed by his twenty five disciples. They proceeded along the road to Tara chanting a hymn which, fifteen

*At Tara, King Laoghaire, surrounded by noblemen and druids,
waited to light the fire. As he was about to do so, he saw flames
lighting the sky across the fields. He was livid with anger.*

centuries later, is still named the Breastplate of St Patrick. When they entered the great banqueting hall of Tara, the missionaries must have been amazed at the sight that confronted them. Used only to formal Roman style, it would have been their first view of a pagan court set out in all its splendour.

The hall at Tara was long and lofty. At the top sat the king surrounded by his courtiers, lawyers, druids, poets, singers and harpists. His queen and daughter sat on his left side. There would have been visitors too from outside – ambassadors from the Mediterranean countries, Levantine merchants, noblemen from Scotland.

Patrick walked up the hall without looking left or right until he reached the king. Then he and his group stopped while everyone waited to see who would speak first.

'Here I am,' said Patrick.

The king took him by the hand and cautiously kissed his cheek. Then they sat down together.

The druids were furious; there was no doubt about that. To be fair to them, they would be out of a job if Patrick succeeded in convincing King Laoghaire. They determined somehow to show up Patrick. They asked the king to demand from Patrick if he could make snow.

Patrick wisely said that that was God's affair, not his. Suddenly, to the amazement of the missionaries, before their eyes they saw snow fall over the sun-filled fields. This was accomplished by the magic of the druids who understood the secrets of nature in a way that was beyond the sophisticated law of the Christians. Patrick did not know what to do. He raised his hand to make the Sign of the Cross over the entranced scene and, to his relief, the snow vanished and the sun shone brightly again.

Then the king asked Patrick to tell the court something about the religion he had brought with him and which he wished the Irish people to accept. Patrick explained to the Court that, instead of having many gods as the Gaels did, Christians believed in only one God. This God of the Christians, Patrick explained, had three personalities: the Father, the Son and the Holy Ghost. The druids, seizing their chance, went into great cackling laughter at this and sneeringly asked Patrick to explain how one God could have three persons.

Patrick prayed to God to give him inspiration so that he might confound the sarcasm of the druids. The Trinity was a mystical idea, not easy to put into words. As he looked down at his feet, thinking furiously, his eye fell on a sprig of shamrock which was growing there. He reached down and picked up a shamrock. 'Here,' he said, taking up the three-leaved flower, 'there is one stem but there are three leaves on it. So it is with the Blessed Trinity. There is one God but three Persons stemming from the same divinity.' Even to this day the shamrock grows only in Ireland.

King Laoghaire was impressed by Patrick. As a result, he gave him permission to preach his gospel in Ireland. He told him he would not himself become a Christian as his father, Niall, had left in his hands the traditions of the Irish people which had been there for many thousands of years, and he would not himself be a party to changing it for another culture or way of life. But he would not stop Patrick preaching his gospel.

So it was at the bidding of this tolerant monarch that Patrick set about his task of converting Ireland to the banner of his Captain Christ.

Patrick's success was astounding. Everywhere in Leinster, people flocked to him to be baptized and become Christians.

His name became known throughout Ireland. His wonderful personality affected every person he met. His eloquent speech attracted a great many. The Irish love fine language and were captivated when Patrick told them of the God of the Christians.

'Our God is the God of all men, the God of heaven and earth, of sea and rivers, of sun and moon and stars, of the lofty mountain and the lowly valleys, the God above heaven and in heaven, and under heaven; He has His dwelling around heaven and earth and sea and all that in them is.

'He inspires all, He quickens all. He dominates all. He supports all.

'He lights the light of the sun, He furnishes the light of the night; He has made springs in the dry land, and has set stars to minister to the greater lights.

'That sun, which we see, by God's command rises daily for our benefit; but it never will reign, nor will its splendour endure; but all those who worship it will pass through wretched misery to punishment; we however, believe in and adore the true Sun, which is Christ, who never shall perish, and neither shall anyone who does His will, but he shall live unto eternity, even as Christ, who reigneth with God the Father Almighty and with the Holy Spirit before all ages, now and for everymore.'

Though Patrick was from a well-known family in Britain, he constantly referred to himself as the slave of Christ.

'I was born a freeman according to the flesh. I am born of a father who was a decurion; but I blush not to say nor do I regret, that I gave up my rank for the profit of others. In short, I am a slave in Christ to a strange nation on account of the unspeakable glory of the Eternal Life which is in Christ Jesus our Lord. And if my own know me not, a Prophet hath no honour in his own country.'

St Patrick Prays in the Mountain

Stories about Patrick are myriad; this one shows the stern side of his character. On one occasion, his disciples criticized him for not asking enough money from his flock. Patrick had an answer. 'It is for charity's sake,' he said, 'that I preach, not charity. For if I asked for money, everything would be given to me and those who follow me would have nothing.' It was Patrick's mission to bring Christianity to Ireland. To accomplish this, he thought it superfluous to ask for money.

Once he went down to meet Angus, the King of Cashel. The kingdom of Cashel lies in the centre of Ireland and the king's palace has always been situated on the top of a mighty rock overlooking the plains of Tipperary. King Angus had expressed a wish to be converted to Christianity. Accordingly, Patrick baptized the king. As he did so, without knowing it, he stuck the point of his crozier right through Angus's foot. Angus did not flinch, thinking the iron point which pierced his foot was part of the ritual of baptism.

When Patrick discovered what he had done, he was horrified. He was also impressed at the endurance that Angus had shown simply because of his wish to become a Christian. As a reward, Patrick promised him that none of his descendants would ever die of wounds.

After he had converted most of Connaught, which is the western province of Ireland, Patrick went on retreat in order to reflect on his life and communicate with God.

He climbed a long stony path to the top of a mountain and there remained in contemplation for forty days and forty nights.

The mountain, now named Croagh Patrick, is on the edge of the Atlantic, almost the last peak of Europe, and to Patrick it must have seemed the last in the world. Remember that at that time America had not yet been discovered.

*Accordingly, Patrick baptized the king. As he did so, without
knowing it, he stuck the point of his crozier right through
Angus's foot. Angus did not flinch, thinking the iron point
which pierced his foot was part of the ritual of baptism.*

From the top of Croagh Patrick, he looked down over the plains of Ireland and could see almost as far as the fields of Meath where he had at first met King Laoghaire and begun his mission to the Irish.

At the time that he made the pilgrimage to Croagh Patrick, Patrick was well over fifty years of age. He suffered greatly on the mountain from hunger and thirst. A storm broke over his head and he thought that he would be washed away by the floods. He was tormented by demons and black ravens sent by the devil to tempt him to despair. But he did not give in.

Presently, an angel came from God to console him. The angel promised him that as a reward for his endurance and for resisting the temptations of the devil, Patrick could make a request to God which would be answered.

Patrick asked that the Irish should hold to the Christian faith to the end of time; that an ocean should drown the country seven years before the Day of Judgment so that the Irish would be spared the horrors of the Last Day; that the Saxons who were now invading Britain should never hold Ireland and that he himself on the Day of Judgment should be allowed to judge his own beloved Irish.

Back in Meath after his return from his pilgrimage, Patrick decided to move to Armagh and establish his bishopric there. Patrick was sad to leave Meath. It is Ireland's richest county, where the cattle graze through endless meadows knee deep in luxuriant grass. It has the name of Royal Meath, not only because it was the seat of the Kings of Ireland but because of the lusciousness of its fields and meadows.

Many a time from the great Hill of Tara, Patrick had looked down on the great plains of Ireland spread before him. Westward was the River Shannon and the broad Atlantic. To the East was the dark blue surface of the Irish Sea.

Presently, an angel came from God to console him. The angel promised him that as a reward for his endurance and for resisting the temptations of the devil, Patrick could make a request to God which would be answered.

It was in Meath that he had received his first welcome in Ireland and it was from Meath that he had set out to convert the rest of the country. He never forgot it.

Patrick was now at the height of his power. His fame had reached Rome and he journeyed there in 441 to pay homage to the new Pope, Leo I. He came back to Ireland bringing with him as a present from the Pope relics of Saints Peter and Paul which he enshrined in the new church that he had built at the Metropolitan See in Armagh. Settled in Armagh, he was able to hand over the administration of the church to auxiliary bishops.

Here is a list of the people who were close to Patrick at this time and formed part of his household:

Sechnall, his bishop.
Mochta, his priest.
Bishop Erc, his judge.
Bishop MacCairthinn, his champion.
Benen, his psalmist.
Coleman of Cell Riada, his chamberlain.
Sinell of Cell Dareis, his bell-ringer.
Athcen of Both Domnaig, his cook.
Presbyter Mescan of Domnach Mescain at Fochain, his brewer.
Presbyter Catan and Presbyter Acan, his two attendants at table.
Odhran of Disert Odrain in Hui Failgi, his charioteer.
Presbyter Manach, his fire-woodman.
Rottan, his cowherd.
His three smiths, namely, MacCecht; Laeben of Domnach Laebain, who made the bell called Findfaidech, and Fortchern in Rath Adine – or, as it is elsewhere, Rath Semni.
His three wrights, Essa, and Bite and Tassach.
His three embroideresses, Lupait and Erc, daughter of Daire, and Cruimtheris in Cengoba.

In the spring of 461, it became clear that this extraordinary man was nearing his end. He was aged seventy-six. His death was a slow one and he suffered a good deal. But he bore his suffering without complaint.

He died on March 17 in the year 461. So great was the love that the noblemen of Ireland bore for Patrick that many clans fought over his body that they would have the honour of burying him in their part of Ireland. In the end, his friends bore his body away to a secret burial place so that even today we are not sure where St Patrick is buried, though it is believed it is in Downpatrick in County Down.

Wherever his body is entombed, he himself survives the grave and he lives on today as surely as if he were alive; Patrick who came to Ireland as a slave and returned as a bishop, determined to make the people he had grown to love, a jewel in the crown of christendom.

THE DRUID AND HIS SOUL

The most powerful people in ancient Ireland were the druids, or priests.

The druids interpreted the movement of the sea, the different shapes of the moon and the seasons of the sun, and claimed to be able to foretell for the king what the gods intended his fate to be. They could cure people of illness. On the other hand, they could weave spells which could result in the death of those against whom they were directed.

They claimed to have power over nature and to be able to bring rain down or induce sunshine by means of their special powers. When the druids spoke, it was thought by the people that they were listening to the voices of the gods transmitting their will through the lips of these chosen people.

There were many famous druids but there was one especially so. People came from all over the world to sit at his feet and listen to his philosophy. He could argue anything. Once he convinced a philosopher from Egypt that black was white. And after he had succeeded in this difficult task, he turned around barefacedly and proved to the man that white was black until, in the end, the unfortunate man did not know whether there was any such thing as colour at all...and maybe there isn't.

The druid was so clever that from time to time he forgot his function as a holy man and one day, somewhat to his surprise, he proved to himself that there was no God.

Worse than this, after proving that there was no God, he went into a veritable ecstasy of denial and finally came out with a cast-iron argument against the existence of the soul.

His argument was so cunning that the king, who really was a religious man, threw up all his beliefs and ordered the people from henceforth not to believe in either God or the existence of the soul. The druid went even further than this: he told the king that he was convinced that logic was the source of all truth. Therefore, if you could not see a thing, it did not exist. The king was so overwhelmed by this syllogism that he immediately summoned the people and ordered them to believe only that which they could see.

One day, the priest was sitting on the edge of a sea-cliff working out a proposition when he found himself talking to a spirit.

The spirit told the druid that he was a very wicked man because he had used his mind to destroy the beliefs of his people; he never listened to the promptings of his heart which was as much a source of truth as his intellect.

'But I was only being logical,' argued the priest.

'Logic is all very well,' replied the angel, 'but you rely upon it alone simply because it satisfies your pride. And now it is too late to argue for you have only a few hours to live.'

The priest was horrified because he was fond of life and he did not want to die just then. Besides, after meeting the angel, his belief in hell was revived and he wanted to avoid going there if he could.

The druid begged the angel to try and arrange that he would have a little more time on earth so that he might end up in purgatory instead of hell and one day enjoy the delights of heaven. Eventually the angel announced that

72

*The spirit told the druid that he was a very wicked man
because he had used his mind to destroy the beliefs of his
people; he never listened to the promptings of his heart which was
as much a source of truth as his intellect.*

the druid could only be saved from hell if he managed to convince the king of the existence of the soul.

The priest got back as quickly as he could to the royal palace and called the king to his chamber. This king was not the one who had first ordered the people to give up their belief in the soul, but his son, who had succeeded him on his death.

The druid was desperate. He had to convince the young king or else burn for ever in hell. But as the young king quite justifiably pointed out, the druid brought him up since he was a boy, to believe only in that which he could see. As he was unable to see the soul, he could not therefore believe in it.

At the end of his tether, the druid asked the young king to assemble the people. When they had gathered on the great plain in front of the palace, the druid knelt down and beseeched the king to draw a knife across his throat.

'Then when you have drawn the knife across my throat, you will see the soul, O King. If you do, will you believe and instruct our people to accept that there is such a thing as a soul?'

The king agreed because he was very disturbed to see the druid's distress. Immediately the king promised the druid smiled happily.

The king drew the knife across the druid's throat, and the druid fell dead at his feet. From his throat fluttered a beautiful white creature that fluttered off into the sunset. This was, the Irish say, the first butterfly. And even today, people in Ireland say that butterflies are souls in purgatory, hovering on the edge of heaven, waiting to get into paradise.

*The king drew the knife across the druid's throat, and the druid
fell dead at his feet. From his throat fluttered a beautiful white
creature that fluttered off into the sunset. This was, the Irish
say, the first butterfly.*

OSSIAN'S RETURN FROM TIR NA N-OG

At all times and among all races there has existed a belief in some form of heaven.

The Irish believe in a place called Tir na n-Og. This means the 'land of the young', where you never grow old. Tir na n-Og existed somewhere beyond the horizon of the sea. Sometimes a white horse could be seen galloping towards the sea's edge. This was some fortunate person who had chosen eternity in that delectable land.

We owe all our knowledge of Tir na n-Og to one man, Ossian, the son of Finn. Ossian was the only person ever to go to Tir na n-Og and come back to Ireland again. Finn, Ossian's father, was the head of a famous band of warriors who lived in Ireland many centuries after Cuchulain, Naisi, Conor and other soldiers and kings we have been reading of.

Finn's people were known as the Fianna. They had very high standards of honour and, as well as being skilful soldiers, were expected to be expert in such unmilitary skills as playing the harp, singing, storytelling and writing poetry.

Ossian was the poet of the Fianna. He recorded the deeds of his soldier companions in poems that often took days to relate but which were full of mellifluous assonance and chiming rhythms.

Ossian's father, Finn, was very proud of his son, not only because he could celebrate the deeds of the Fianna in superb verse but because he was the most handsome of the Fianna. He had curls of red-golden hair and a perfectly chiselled nose which was placed between two eyes of the most subtle colour of green.

One day, the Fianna were hunting in Killarney, in the south of Ireland, when they saw, coming across the lake, what looked to be a travelling cloud. When it drew near, they could see that it was a very beautiful girl astride a white horse that was galloping in some magic way over the water towards them. The horse came up on the shore of the lake, shaking the water from its legs. Now they could see the beautiful princess who rode upon it. Her hair was gold, but it shone like silver and her face was not big-featured like many of the queens and princesses of Ireland, beautiful as they were, but exquisitely small with a little nose pushing its way up over lips that looked like an early rosebud.

This splendid girl had a marvellous cloak that seemed to glow and twinkle as she sat on her horse looking down at the Fianna. Finn, who was never really startled at anything, said calmly enough:

'Who are you, beautiful one, who comes galloping over water?'

The lady said her name was Niamh and that she had come from Tir na n-Og where her father was king. The Fianna gasped for they knew of Tir na n-Og, of course, but had never seen or met anyone from there before.

Then Niamh said something which made Finn very sad indeed. She told him that she had paid this visit to the land of mortals, travelling thousands of miles,

77

They saw, coming across the lake, what looked to be a travelling cloud. When it drew near, they could see that it was a very beautiful girl astride a white horse that was galloping in some magic way over the water towards them.

because she had fallen in love with his son, Ossian. She had seen him on one of her previous visits one day when he was out hunting, sprinting through the morning fields, his red hair streaming in the wind and his white limbs glistening in the dew.

Finn told her that she might speak to Ossian if she wanted to. When Niamh saw Ossian, her face lit up, her eyes gleamed and immediately she began to tell him of the wonders of the land she had come from.

He would have everything he wanted, she told him. Castles, kingdoms, service, horses for hunting, hounds for racing, musicians to play for him and bards to sing for him. He would have the costliest garments woven from silk and fur, and drink and food would be available in such abundance and variety as he could never conceive.

Always the trees would be in bloom in Tir na n-Og. There was no winter there. He could forget fog and frost and snow for he would never know them again.

Above all, he would never grow old. He would not know sickness or disease. He would remain as he was now for ever. Time stood still in Tir na n-Og.

When Finn saw that Ossian was becoming fascinated by the story Niamh was telling him, he began to feel worried for he did not want to see his son leave and go to this mysterious land.

Ossian said to his father, 'Don't worry if I go with Niamh. I shall remain only for a short time. After all, no one has been to Tir na n-Og and come back, and it is only proper that a member of the Fianna should be the first to do so.'

Finn's eyes filled with tears when he heard this because he knew in some way that if Ossian went to Tir na n-Og he should see him no more.

The Land of Tir na n–Og

Ossian mounted the back of the white horse, behind Niamh, and together they swept over the land till they reached the ocean. Then, the horse stepped as lightly over the waves as if he were moving on the Curragh racecourse itself.

It proved a glorious journey, galloping into the enchanted castles of the sunset, behind the most beautiful girl Ossian had ever set eyes upon, his face buried in the golden hair that cascaded down her back.

This journey continued for hours until they came to land. The sun had gone down and it seemed as if they had galloped through the sunset.

As soon as they landed on this new place, the sky glowed with a bright, translucent light, more radiant than Ossian had ever seen before. They passed on their white horse through fields of apple trees, almond trees and orange trees, and everywhere they could see handsome people, men and women, laughing and singing, and telling tales together. The houses were not like the dwelling places Ossian had known at home. Each house was decorated with sparkling diamonds and jewels. He could see that the floors were covered by rich carpets, woven with marvellous designs.

Magnificent as these places were, they were nothing to the sight he would see when he reached Niamh's father's palace. It rose hundreds of feet in the air and looked as he approached it to be a mass of bristling turrets. It was as if twenty castles had been put together and turned into a single one.

As they approached the king's court, through long corridors of the palace, the scent of peach trees and orange trees filtered through the rooms and incense rose from thuribles on the floor. Niamh's father was seated on the throne, next to his queen. Niamh ran up to her father who embraced her. He was enchanted that she had

'Don't worry if I go with Niamh,' Ossian said to his father. 'I shall remain only for a short time. After all, no one has been to Tir na n-Og and come back, and it is only proper that a member of the Fianna should be the first to do so.'

It proved a glorious journey, galloping into the enchanted castles of the sunset, behind the most beautiful girl Ossian had ever set eyes upon, his face buried in the golden hair that cascaded down her back.

obtained at last the desire of her heart.

Thus did Ossian go from Ireland with Niamh and live with her in Tir na n-Og. He forgot one thing, though. Time did not exist in that enchanted land. A year passed like an hour. A hundred years like a day.

One day after he had been some time there, he asked a druid at the court to count the number of days he had spent in this new country. To Ossian it seemed he had stayed away from Ireland no more then ten years. He was horrified when he learnt from the druid that he had been over three hundred years in Tir na n-Og.

His face had not changed, neither had his body, from the day he left Ireland. Each day had passed without flaw or blemish. But the years had slipped by.

Ossian was suddenly brokenhearted when he realized that his father and the Fianna must now be long dead. He went to Niamh and begged her to return to Ireland even for a short time. Niamh saw how much it meant to him and she agreed that Ossian might go. But she warned him that the country was changed from the time he had been there. A holy man, it was said, had come from outside Ireland and given the people a new religion which had replaced the warrior creed that the Fianna had adhered to in Ireland. There was one thing she warned him he must not do: he should never dismount from the saddle of his horse and put a foot on the soil of Ireland. If this happened, he would never see her again.

Ossian mounted the white horse on which he had come to Tir na n-Og and set out into the sunset, back across the path he had first come when he journeyed with Niamh across the water.

During the journey, they ran into a fearful thunderstorm. The sea rolled beneath them. Great waves of brown seaweed tangled in the horse's legs. All around, the sky seemed to have split open as rain poured down and lightning lit the sky.

But Ossian's white steed bore him onwards.

The Return

Eventually, after three days and three nights, he landed in Ireland. Ossian was full of joy to be once again on the soil of his native land.

But he was baffled by what he saw in the first few hours he spent. The men and women seemed to have got smaller. Even the animals were not as big as they used to be.

Nowhere could he find the castles and hunting lodges where the Fianna had lived. Occasionally he came across people who had heard of the Fianna. It was only in books and through sagas that they were remembered. They were now, it seemed, regarded as pagan warriors, without the gift of the new religion this stranger had brought to Ireland. Ossian questioned people vigorously about Manannan, Lir and Lu and the other Celtic gods the Fianna had prayed to. A look of fear came over people's faces when he mentioned these names and he was told he must not speak of them now as the priests had condemned the old gods, smashed the statues, refused to· allow people to take part in pagan worship.

As he rode along the island, Ossian became more and more dispirited. He decided he would go and visit Glen na Smole, the Valley of the Thrushes. This was a favourite hunting place of the Fianna. Those who know Ireland today will recognize the name Glen na Smole. It is only about five miles from Dublin City. At the foot of the glen, there are two superb lakes that reflect the blue of the sky, and on each side for miles around stretch mountains covered in purple heather and yellow gorse.

As he rode through this former playground of the Fianna, Ossian was thinking of the many hours he had spent there with his comrades and of his father whom he would never see again.

He noticed as he went along a group of men trying to move a huge stone from the ground. Their muscles were bulging from the effort and their backs were gleaming in

The sea rolled beneath them. Great waves of brown seaweed
tangled in the horse's legs. All around, the sky seemed to have
split open as rain poured down and lightning lit the sky.

the sun from sweat. They had not the strength to lift the stone completely off the ground though they were trying hard to do so.

Ossian was so contemptuous of what passed now for Irishmen that he rode up to the group and told them he would lift the stone for them. They stood away from it and looked up at him with scorn, not believing that he could move it at all.

Ossian reached down from his saddle and grasped the stone in both hands, and, gathering it into his breast, lifted it from the ground. The men around gasped when they saw what he had done for sixteen of them had not been able to move it. Ossian asked them sarcastically where they wanted to put the stone and, when they pointed to a place, he braced himself to throw it towards the spot. As he raised the stone to despatch it, his left stirrup broke with the extra weight of the stone and Ossian slipped off the horse to the ground.

As soon as he touched the ground, the horrified onlookers saw this handsome youth transformed into a crippled old man, trembling with age, and barely able to speak.

Niamh had told him that she would never see him again if his feet touched the soil of Ireland, and so it had come to pass.

The white horse turned, shook his head and galloped off over the glen, seeming, as he crossed the mountains to vanish into the sky.

This is how Ossian spent his last years. The only man who had ever come back from Tir na n-Og. It was a sad end indeed for the warrior poet of the Fianna.

*The white horse turned, shook his head and galloped off over
the glen, seeming, as he crossed the mountains, to vanish into the sky.*

THE COUNTESS CATHLEEN O'SHEA

At one time there was a dreadful famine in Ireland and many people were starving to death. It was a pity to see children by the roadside as thin as scarecrows, holding out their hands to passers by for a crust of bread or a drop of milk that would keep them alive. In winter it became worse because the poor had no warm food inside them to protect them against the frost and snow.

About this time two merchants began to travel about the countryside. It wasn't clear at first what business they were about as they didn't buy or sell goods but contented themselves with moving amongst the people watching and noting their pitiful condition but showing no sign of pity at all. Soon certain folk began to report that they had seen the merchants at night flying towards the moon in the form of owls. It was said that they had come from the Land Under the Wave and had been sent by the Evil One. Now in daytime when they went about their business it was noticeable that they had dark glittering eyes and that they kept their hands always gloved because as some thought they had talons instead of fingers.

Soon certain folk began to report that they had seen the
merchants at night flying towards the moon in the form of owls.
It was said that they had come from the Land Under the Wave
and had been sent by the Evil One.

89

*Many thousands were dying at this time and more were on the
point of death. The thought of money with which they could buy
food sent the creatures hurrying in great numbers to see what they
could exchange for the merchants' gold.*

90

One day it became clear what they were about. The pair of merchants spread out a Persian rug on the ground in the square in a big town. They announced they would pay sums of gold to people who would sell them what they wanted.

Many thousands were dying at this time and more were on the point of death. The thought of money with which they could buy food sent the creatures hurrying in great numbers to see what they could exchange for the merchants' gold. Eventually there was a tremendous crowd present. Then the merchants announced that they had come to trade for souls. They would give gold in exchange, but strictly in accordance with the value of the soul. The two men with their watchful eyes took out a scroll and from it they read their terms:

> Old people who had souls to sell would get fifty pieces of gold.
> A middle-aged woman if she were handsome would get two hundred pieces, if she were ugly, one hundred.
> A young man or woman were worth three hundred pieces of gold each. And a virgin would fetch five hundred pieces.

Now its no reflection on the people to say that many of them were tempted with this enticing offer. God help the creatures, they were half mad anyway with the suffering and the sight of their families and relatives dying around them. First one and then another put up their emaciated hands and said they would like to talk to the men from Under the Wave. After that many more followed. Soon there was a queue that stretched right through the township waiting to deal with the merchants.

Now at this time in Ireland there lived a beautiful countess, Cathleen O'Shea. She lived alone in a grand mansion by the side of a green lake and surrounded by beautiful woods. She was a tall woman of great beauty, with sapphire eyes. When she walked people said it was like a swan sailing on a lake so graceful were her movements and so little disturbance did she put on the other parts of her body. Once the countess Cathleen had been married to a great prince from Poland but he had drowned in the lake in the middle of a storm. She had taken back her maiden name and now lived alone like a nun in her cell but surrounded by great wealth and beautiful objects.

The countess was broken-hearted at the suffering of the people around her. When she heard that not only their bodies were perishing, but their souls would be endangered for ever as well if they sold them to get food, she decided she would do everything in her power to stop the Evil One from recruiting new inhabitants for his region.

She called her servant in one day and asked him to make a list of all her property.

'How much have I got,' she asked him when he came in to her carrying the account books piled up in his arms.

'You have five hundred thousand pounds of gold.'

'How is that made up, in money or in land?'

'You have diamonds, jewellery, forests, lakes and ranches to the value of four hundred thousand. The rest is your house and gold.'

The generous countess ordered her servant to sell everything except her mansion and keep the gold bullion so that she would have enough to live on. The rest was to be given to the poor to buy food.

As soon as the news got around that the countess was distributing her money the people were overjoyed. It was clear now that there would be enough money available to stop the famine until next year's crop would come around.

The two merchants from Under the Wave were furious. There were no more souls for sale. The people

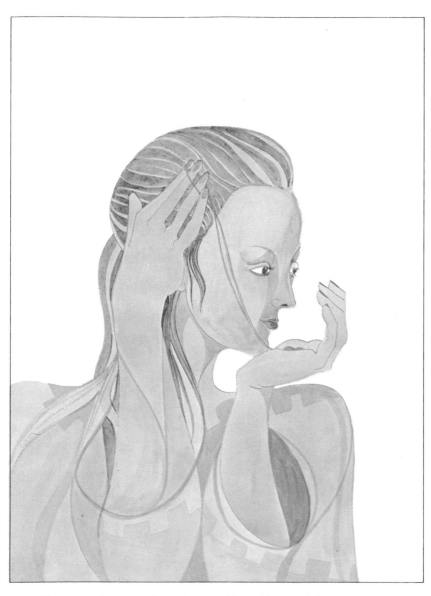

She was a tall woman of great beauty, with sapphire eyes. When she walked people said it was like a swan sailing on a lake so graceful were her movements and so little disturbance did she put on the other parts of her body.

had no need of evil gold now that it had been replaced by the bounty of Countess Cathleen. The merchants by night flew against the moon and croaked in fury, whilst by day in human guise they tramped the road. But they could come to no solution to satisfy their master, the Evil One.

At last they decided that if they could steal the countess's gold she would be penniless. Then there would be no one to help the people if another famine came.

One night the two stole into the Countess Cathleen's mansion and cast a spell on her. She tried to cry out the name of God which would have dissolved the demons but they had paralysed her throat so that she was unable to speak. After a lot of rooting around they found the gold and took it away. It was short work for them after that to poison the crops so that the following year there was another famine. Now the people were dying in even greater numbers and there was no one to hand out money or food to them. The merchants rubbed their taloned hands in anticipation of all the souls they would have to bring back to their master.

Then the countess did something that no one would have thought of. She decided to sell her own soul if the merchants would give her enough money for it so that her people wouldn't have to starve nor sell themselves to eternal damnation.

Needless to say the two merchants were astonished when this beautiful woman approached them.

'What price will you give for a soul?'

'It depends on what class of a soul it is. The soul like a diamond is valued by its transparency.'

'How much is my soul worth?'

'Yours, beautiful lady?'

'Yes, mine.'

The two blackguards were so delighted at the thought of what power this would give them that they offered her a million golden pieces. The Countess

An angel appeared over the crowd and told them that Cathleen was not in hell but in heaven. She had laid down her soul that her people might have eternal life and God had declared the sale null and void.

Cathleen knew that this would be sufficient to save all her people no matter what the demons might do. She accepted though she knew she would have to face an eternity of hell.

As soon as the countess got the money she had it distributed to the people and there was great rejoicing once again. Now they knew there would be no more hunger or suffering in Ireland in their lifetime. But none of them knew the awful price that Countess Cathleen O'Shea had paid. The only one that knew that was her devoted servant whom she had told when she asked him to distribute the money.

It was her servant who found her cold and dead in the mansion one morning and went out and told the people the news.

When it was heard round the countryside that the countess was dead there was great lamentation. But when the servant told the people how the countess sold her soul to get money for them, multitudes came and knelt by her grave to ask her forgiveness.

As they did an angel appeared over the crowd and told them that Cathleen was not in hell but in heaven. She had laid down her soul that her people might have eternal life and God had declared the sale null and void. So the demons lost after all. The people of Ireland were saved and Cathleen, as Ireland's greatest poet has said, now 'walks on the floor of peace'.